FUNdamental Experiments

Magnets

by Ellen Lawrence

Consultants:

Suzy Gazlay, MA
Recipient, Presidential Award for Excellence in Science Teaching

Kimberly Brenneman, PhD
National Institute for Early Education Research, Rutgers University, New Brunswick, New Jersey

BEARPORT
PUBLISHING

New York, New York

Credits

Cover, © Krasyuk/Thinkstock, © Olga Oliynyk/Thinkstock, © thieury/Shutterstock, and © Rob Hyrons/Shutterstock; 3, © CoraMax/Shutterstock and Matthew Cole/Shutterstock; 4L, © Rubberball/Superstock; 4C, © Szekeres Szabolcs/Shutterstock; 4R, Sashkin/Shutterstock; 5, © yavuzunlu/Shutterstock, © molaruso/Shutterstock, © April Cat/Shutterstock, © Fotovika/Shutterstock, and © CoraMax/Shutterstock; 6–7, © CoraMax/Shutterstock, © Peshkov Daniil/Shutterstock, © Aaron Amat/Shutterstock, © JirkaBursik/Shutterstock, © sNike/Shutterstock, © Igor Kovalchuk/Shutterstock, © Eldad Carin/Shutterstock, and © Oez/Shutterstock; 8–9, © CoraMax/Shutterstock and © Matthew Cole/Shutterstock; 10–11, © Peshkov Daniil/Shutterstock, © Kitch Bain/Shutterstock, © Matthew Cole/Shutterstock, and © CoraMax/Shutterstock; 12–13, © CoraMax/Shutterstock, © Ruth Owen, © Matthew Cole/Shutterstock, and © Evgeny Karandaev/Shutterstock; 14–15, © Piotr Krzeslak/Shutterstock, © CoraMax/Shutterstock, © Ruth Owen, © Ilona Baha/Shutterstock, and © Danny Smythe/Shutterstock; 16–17, © CoraMax/Shutterstock, © zebicho/Shutterstock, and © Alexey A. Belikov/Shutterstock; 18–19, © CoraMax/Shutterstock, © Matthew Cole/Shutterstock, and © Peshkov Daniil/Shutterstock; 20–21, © CoraMax/Shutterstock, © Matthew Cole/Shutterstock, © Peshkov Daniil/Shutterstock, © Kitch Bain/Shutterstock, © Piotr Krzeslak/Shutterstock, © Ruth Owen, © zebicho/Shutterstock, and © Alexey A. Belikov/Shutterstock; 22TL, © Blue Jean Images/Superstock; 22TR, © Blend Images/Superstock; 22BL, © n. yanchuk/Shutterstock; 22BR, © worradirek/Shutterstock; 23, © Ruth Owen, © April Cat/Shutterstock, © Rubberball/Superstock, © CoraMax/Shutterstock, and © Matthew Cole/Shutterstock.

Publisher: Kenn Goin
Senior Editor: Joyce Tavolacci
Creative Director: Spencer Brinker
Design: Emma Randall
Photo Researcher: Ruby Tuesday Books Ltd.

Library of Congress Cataloging-in-Publication Data in process at time of publication (2015)
Library of Congress Control Number: 2014013737
ISBN-13: 978-1-62724-312-4 (library binding)

For more information, write to Bearport Publishing Company, Inc., 45 West 21st Street, Suite 3B, New York, NY 10010. Printed in the United States of America.

10 9 8 7 6 5 4 3 2 1

Contents

Let's Investigate Magnets

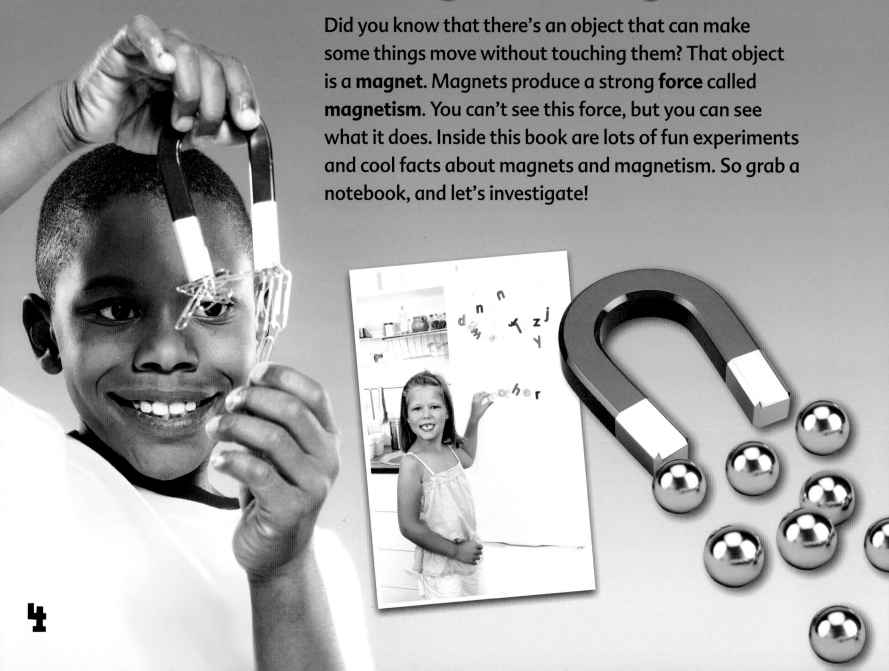

Did you know that there's an object that can make some things move without touching them? That object is a **magnet**. Magnets produce a strong **force** called **magnetism**. You can't see this force, but you can see what it does. Inside this book are lots of fun experiments and cool facts about magnets and magnetism. So grab a notebook, and let's investigate!

4

Check It Out!

A magnet produces an area of magnetic force around itself called a **magnetic field**. It's not possible to see or touch the magnetic field. However, you can tell that it's there because when certain objects enter the field, you can feel a pulling force between the magnet and the objects. Let's check it out.

Find a magnet to use for your investigations.
Magnets come in lots of different shapes and sizes.

 bar magnet

 ring magnet

horseshoe magnet

1. Hold the magnet about 12 inches (31 cm) from a refrigerator, washing machine, or dishwasher.

2. Slowly move the magnet toward the object. What happens when the magnet gets close to it? What do you feel?

3. Now repeat this investigation on a wooden door or window frame. What happens?

4. What types of objects do you think are **attracted** to a magnet?

What kinds of materials can a magnet attract?

When you placed the magnet close to a metal object, such as a refrigerator, you felt a pulling force between the two objects. That's because the refrigerator door is made of metal and the magnet and the door were attracted to each other. There was no attraction, however, between the magnet and a wooden object. This is because magnetic force does not attract all **materials**. Let's find out which materials are attracted to a magnet.

You will need:

- A metal paper clip
- A stone
- A dime
- A stick
- A metal spoon
- A piece of aluminum foil
- A metal screw
- A plastic toy
- A notebook and pencil
- A magnet

 Gather together the objects listed in the green box. Line them up in a row on a table, except for the magnet.

▶ **Which objects do you think will be attracted to the magnet?**

Write your **predictions** in your notebook.

Slowly move the magnet toward the first object.

▶ **What did the object do?**

▶ **Was there an attraction between the magnet and the object?**

Record what happened in your notebook.

 Move the magnet toward each of the other objects, one by one. Write down what happens.

▶ **Which of the objects were attracted to the magnet?**

▶ **What do these objects have in common?**

(To learn more about this investigation and find the answers to the questions, see pages 20–21.)

7

Can a magnet push or pull another magnet?

When two magnets are placed near each other, they can create two different kinds of forces. They may push away, or **repel**, each other, or they may pull each other closer together. So why do magnets sometimes push or pull? Let's investigate!

You will need:

- Two bar magnets labeled A and B
- A notebook and pencil

Take one of the magnets and examine it. You will see that its ends are marked with the letters N and S. The ends of the magnet are known as its poles. The N stands for "north pole" and the S stands for "south pole."

Put both of the magnets on a table about six inches (15 cm) apart. Position magnet A so that its north pole faces the south pole of magnet B.

Now slowly push magnet B toward magnet A.

▶ **What happens to magnet A?**

Now place the magnets six inches (15 cm) apart with their north poles facing each other.

▶ **What do you think will happen to magnet A when magnet B gets closer?**

Write your prediction in your notebook.

Then slowly push magnet B toward magnet A.

▶ **Does your prediction match what happened?**

Next, place the magnets six inches (15 cm) apart with their south poles facing each other.

▶ **What do you think will happen when you push magnet B closer to magnet A?**

Write your prediction in your notebook, and then test it.

▶ **What effect is magnet B having on magnet A?**

▶ **How do you make a magnet pull another magnet?**

▶ **How do you make a magnet push another magnet?**

(To learn more about this investigation and find the answers to the questions, see pages 20–21.)

9

How large is a magnet's magnetic field?

Every magnet produces a different-sized magnetic field around itself. The more powerful a magnet is, the larger its magnetic field will be. It's not possible to see the magnetic field around a magnet. It is possible, however, to find out how far its magnetic field can reach. Let's investigate!

You will need:

- A wooden ruler
- A metal paper clip
- A bar magnet
- A notebook and pencil

Put a ruler on a table. Place a paper clip alongside one end of the ruler. The end of the paper clip should line up with the number zero at the end of the ruler. Place a magnet at the other end of the ruler.

▶ If you push the magnet toward the paper clip, how close do you think it will get before the paper clip is attracted to the magnet?

Write your prediction in your notebook.

2 Hold the ruler in place with one hand. With the other hand, slowly slide the magnet toward the paper clip. The moment the paper clip moves, stop sliding the magnet. In your notebook, record where on the ruler you stopped the magnet.

3 Try the investigation using the magnet's other pole, or end.

▶ **How many inches do you think the magnet will move this time?**

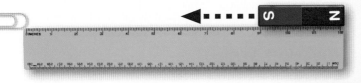

Write your prediction in your notebook. Then test it.

4 Now, try the investigation with just one of the magnet's poles resting against the ruler. Line up the end of the paper clip with zero, but place it so that it's not touching the ruler. Predict what you think will happen when you move the magnet closer to the paper clip. Then flip the magnet to test the other pole.

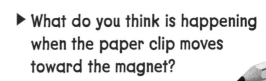

▶ **What do you think is happening when the paper clip moves toward the magnet?**

▶ **How many inches does the magnet's magnetic field reach at its poles? How about at its sides?**

▶ **What does the paper clip do if the magnet is standing on one of its poles?**

(To learn more about this investigation and find the answers to the questions, see pages 20–21.)

Can a magnet's magnetic field pass through materials?

You've already discovered how far the magnetic field of a magnet can reach. What will happen, however, if paper or another type of material is placed between a magnet and a metal object? Will the magnet's magnetic field pass through certain materials?

You will need:

- A sheet of paper
- Six metal paper clips
- A magnet
- A notebook and pencil
- A piece of thick cardboard
- Aluminum foil
- A small ceramic or plastic plate

 Hold a sheet of paper in one hand with your fingers spread out so it's flat. Place some paper clips on top of the paper. With your other hand, hold a magnet under the paper and touch the paper beneath the paper clips.

▶ Can the magnet move the paper clips?

Now, try the experiment again. This time, place the paper clips on top of the cardboard.

▶ **Do you think the magnet's magnetic field will pass through the cardboard?**

Write your prediction in your notebook. Place the magnet under the cardboard and try to move the paper clips.

 Repeat the experiment with aluminum foil and then with the plate. You can also try the experiment using this book.

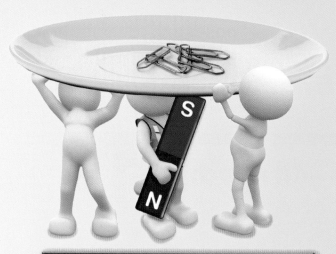

Write down everything you observed in your notebook.

▶ **Was the magnet able to move the paper clips through each of the materials?**

(To learn more about this investigation and find the answers to the questions, see pages 20–21.)

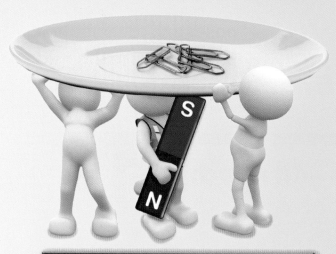

Do magnets work in water?

You discovered that your magnet's magnetic field can work through paper and other materials. Is it possible, though, for a magnet to work underwater? In this next investigation, let's find out if metal objects can be pulled through water by a magnet!

You will need:

- Six metal paper clips
- A small glass
- Water
- A notebook and pencil
- A magnet

 Put six paper clips in the bottom of a glass.

 Slowly fill the glass with water.

3 Make sure the paper clips are lying at the bottom of the glass.

▶ Do you think it's possible to remove the paper clips from the water using a magnet placed on the outside of the glass?

Write your prediction in your notebook.

 4 Hold a magnet against the glass, close to the paper clips.

▶ What happens to the paper clips?

▶ What can you do to make the paper clips move?

▶ Can you use the magnet to remove the paper clips from the glass?

Write down in your notebook everything you observed.

▶ What have you learned about water and magnetic fields in this investigation?

(To learn more about this investigation and find the answers to the questions, see pages 20–21.)

Can a magnet make other objects magnetic?

Magnetism is a force found in nature. However, people can also make objects that are magnetic. Your magnet, for example, was produced in a factory. Could this magnet pass on its magnetism to another metal object? Let's investigate!

You will need:

- A pair of stainless-steel scissors
- Some metal paper clips
- A magnet
- A notebook and pencil
- An adult helper

1 Begin by testing whether your scissors have a magnetic field. Hold the metal blades of a pair of closed scissors next to some paper clips. Be very careful while you're holding the scissors.

▶ What happens to the paper clips?

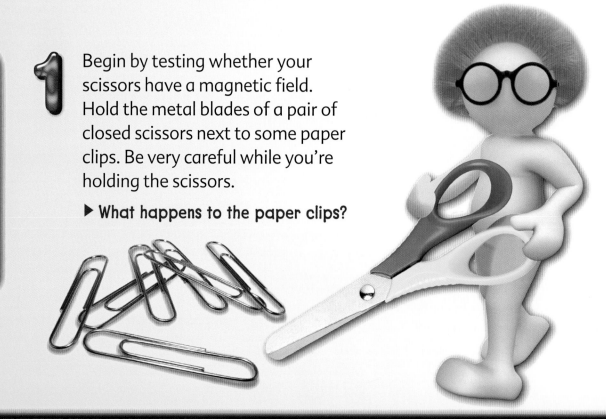

2 Ask an adult helper to rub your magnet against the blades of the scissors for about one minute.

▶ **What do you think will happen now if you hold the scissors close to the paper clips?**

Record your prediction in your notebook.

3 Hold the scissors close to the paper clips.

▶ **Are the paper clips attracted to the scissors now?**

▶ **Does what happened match your prediction?**

▶ **What has happened to the scissors?**

(To learn more about this investigation and find the answers to the questions, see pages 20–21.)

How can magnetism make a paper clip float in the air?

A magnet's magnetic field cannot be seen. As a result, you can use a magnet and some thread to make a paper clip look as if it's floating in the air. Of course, the paper clip is held in the air because it is attracted to the magnet. To your friends, however, it will look like magic!

You will need:

- A pair of scissors
- Thread
- A table
- Masking tape
- A metal paper clip
- A magnet

 Use a pair of scissors to cut a piece of thread about ten inches (25 cm) long.

 Tape one end of the thread to the table using masking tape.

 Tie the other end of the thread to a paper clip and then place the paper clip on the table.

Hold the magnet close enough to the paper clip so that the magnet can move it, but don't let the two objects touch each other.

Slowly lift the paper clip without letting the magnet touch it until the thread is standing straight up. Now try to keep the paper clip floating in mid-air.

It looks like magic, but it's actually science!

Write down in your notebook everything you did.

Use these words in your description of what happened:

- magnetic field

- attracted

- magnetism

(To learn more about this investigation and find the answers to the questions, see pages 20–21.)

Discovery Time

It's fun to investigate how magnets work. Now, let's check out all the amazing things we discovered.

Pages 6–7

What kinds of materials can a magnet attract?

The objects that were attracted to the magnet were all made out of metal. Not all metals are attracted to magnets, though. Iron is a type of metal that's attracted to magnets. Steel is metal that contains iron and is attracted to magnets. If the paper clip, screw, and spoon were attracted to your magnet, that's because they are made from steel that contains iron. The stick, aluminum foil, stone, dime, and plastic toy were not attracted to the magnet because they don't contain iron.

Pages 8–9

Can a magnet push or pull another magnet?

When the south pole of one magnet is near the north pole of another magnet, the magnets are pulled together. When the north poles of two magnets are close together, they will repel each other. The same is true for the two south poles of two magnets.

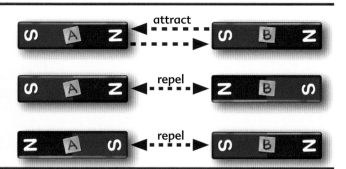

Pages 10–11

How large is a magnet's magnetic field?

When the paper clip moves toward the magnet, it is moving because the magnet's magnetic field has reached the paper clip and is pulling it. For example, if the paper clip moved when it was two inches (5 cm) from the magnet, this shows that the magnetic field reaches two inches (5 cm) beyond the end of the magnet. The sides of a bar magnet may not be as powerful as its poles. In fact, when the magnet's side was facing the paper clip, the paper clip may have been attracted to the end of the magnet and not its side. That's because a magnet's magnetic field is stronger at its north and south poles.

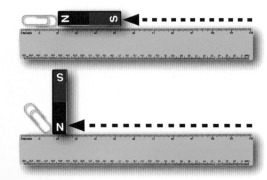

Can a magnet's magnetic field pass through materials?

Pages 12–13

Your magnet was probably able to move the paper clips through the paper, cardboard, and foil. It might also have moved the paper clips through the plate and this book. That's because the magnet's magnetic field could pass through the materials. Even though there was another material between your magnet and the paper clips, the paper clips were still inside the magnetic field. The other material couldn't block the magnetic field. Perhaps the paper clips didn't move, though, when you placed a thick object between them and the magnet. If this happened, it was because the paper clips were now outside of your magnet's magnetic field.

Do magnets work in water?

Pages 14–15

When a magnet is held against a glass of water, the paper clips are attracted to the magnet. If the magnet is slowly moved up the glass, the paper clips move, too. Then they can be lifted out of the water. This shows that a magnet's magnetic field can work through glass and through water.

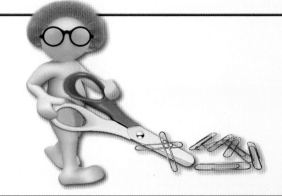

Can a magnet make other objects magnetic?

Pages 16–17

When the magnet was rubbed against the scissor's blades, the magnet passed on its magnetism to the metal scissors. The scissors will now have their own magnetic field for a short while and will attract paper clips. That's why when you held the scissors close to the paper clips, the scissors and paper clips were attracted to each other.

How can magnetism make a paper clip float in the air?

Pages 18–19

When the magnet's magnetic field reached the paper clip, the magnet and paper clip were attracted to each other because of magnetism. As long as the paper clip is inside the magnet's magnetic field, it will stay up in the air and appear as if it's floating.

Magnets in Your World

Magnets aren't just great fun to use in science experiments.
They can also be very useful in everyday life.

1. Open the refrigerator door. Now gently close the door and notice how it feels. You didn't have to push hard or turn a handle to shut the door tight.

▶ **What do you think could be holding the refrigerator door closed?**

2. A magnet is attracted to the metal door of a refrigerator.

▶ **What happens, however, if a note or picture is placed between the magnet and the refrigerator door?**

3. This diary contains two magnets.

▶ **How do you think the magnets are used?**

magnet

4. Very large, powerful magnets are often used in junkyards.

▶ **What job do you think the magnets perform?**

Answers: 1. The door of a refrigerator uses magnets to keep it closed tight. There are magnets on the edge of the door that line up with magnets on the frame inside the refrigerator. 2. The magnet is still attracted to the refrigerator door. That's because paper and many other materials cannot block a magnet's magnetic field. 3. One magnet is on the front cover of the diary. The other is on the clasp. The magnets are attracted to each other and hold the diary tightly closed. 4. Magnets are used to lift and move pieces of heavy metal, such as old cars. They are also used to separate metal junk made from iron out of junk made from other materials, such as plastic and wood.

Science Words

attracted (uh-TRAKT-id) pulled together by the force of magnetism

force (FORSS) something that causes movement, such as a pull or a push

magnet (MAG-nit) an object that produces a strong force, called magnetism, around itself

magnetic field (mag-NET-ik FEELD) a force around a magnet that pushes or pulls metal objects and other magnets

magnetism (MAG-nuh-tiz-uhm) a force produced by a magnet that attracts metal objects to the magnet

materials (muh-TIHR-ee-uhlz) any substance from which things are made; for example, metal, wood, and paper are all materials

predictions (pri-DIK-shuhnz) guesses that something will happen in a certain way; they are often based on facts a person knows or something a person has observed

repel (ri-PEL) to push away

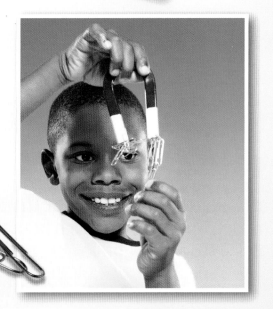

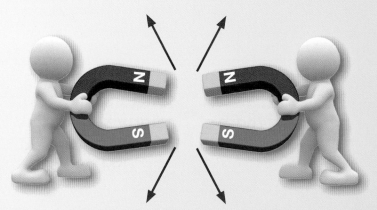

Index

Read More

Ballard, Carol. *Exploring Magnets and Springs (How Does Science Work?)*. New York: PowerKids Press (2008).

Guillain, Charlotte. *Magnets (Investigate)*. Chicago: Heinemann (2008).

Vogel, Julia. *Push and Pull! (Learn About Magnets)*. North Mankato, MN: Child's World (2011).

Learn More Online

To learn more about magnets, visit
www.bearportpublishing.com/FundamentalExperiments

About the Author

Ellen Lawrence lives in the United Kingdom. Her favorite books to write are those about nature and animals. In fact, the first book Ellen bought for herself, when she was six years old, was the story of a gorilla named Patty Cake that was born in New York's Central Park Zoo.